Communities and Technology

Printed in Mexico

ISBN-13: 978-0-15-367353-5
ISBN-10: 0-15-367353-2

3 4 5 6 7 8 9 10   050   13 12 11 10 09 08

SCHOOL PUBLISHERS

Visit *The Learning Site!* www.harcourtschool.com

Technology Changes Communities

READ TO FIND OUT How does technology change where people live?

Technology changes the ways people build. **Technology** is the use of new tools and new ideas. In 1885, people used steel and iron to build the first skyscraper. As elevators became safer, people could build taller skyscrapers.

People use new kinds of technology to build skyscrapers.

Many people drive to and from work on highways.

Technology changes where people live. In the 1800s, trains made it easier for people and goods to travel. Towns were soon built along train tracks.

In the 1900s, many people began to drive cars. Communities grew up near new roads. People could live farther from work.

READING CHECK ŏ **GENERALIZE** How does technology change where people live?

Our Economy and Technology

READ TO FIND OUT **How do people use technology?**

Technology helps people make, buy, and sell things to one another. This is part of an economy. An **economy** is the way a country or a community makes and uses goods and services.

Some people use machines to make goods in factories. **Goods** are things that can be bought or sold. Farmers use technology to grow plants.

Tennis balls are goods.

Doctors help people stay well.

Doctors and banks use technology to give services. A **service** is work that someone does for someone else. Doctors keep people well. They use X-ray machines. Banks keep people's money safe. The workers use computers to keep track of it.

Technology helps workers make more goods quickly. Machines make goods faster and easier.

READING CHECK **MAIN IDEA AND DETAILS How do people use technology?**

Leaders in Technology

READ TO FIND OUT **What do inventors do?**

Communities have changed with ideas and inventions. **Inventions** are things that are made for the first time. Inventors are people who make these new things.

Some new ideas and tools change the way people do things. Josephine Cochran came up with the idea for a dishwasher. It made cleaning up after meals easier and faster.

Josephine Cochran invented a dishwasher in 1886.

Alexander Graham Bell's telephone

Some inventions made communication faster. **Communication** is the sharing of information. Alexander Graham Bell invented the telephone in 1876. For the first time, people could talk to friends who were far away.

In 1971, Ray Tomlinson sent e-mail over the Internet. The **Internet** links computers around the world.

READING CHECK MAIN IDEA AND DETAILS **What do inventors do?**

Communication Around the World

READ TO FIND OUT **How do people get news?**

Long ago, sending letters was the only way to communicate with people who lived far away. It could take weeks for a letter to reach a person.

Today, people get news in many ways. People can still send letters, but telephones and e-mail are much faster.

Internet cafés help people get the news.

Newspapers give people information.

People get news in other ways. They read papers. They listen to radios and watch television. They use fax machines. These machines send messages and pictures over telephone lines.

Some children in Australia live very far from their school. They join their class by radio and computer. This is called "the school of the air."

READING CHECK ☼ **GENERALIZE** How do people get news?

Global Technology

READ TO FIND OUT **How do countries ship goods?**

People around the world use technology. They use it in their homes and schools. Technology helps people get news and go places. They use it to make, buy, and sell goods. They use it to move goods, too.

Communities and countries buy goods from one another. Japan sells cars to many countries. The United States sells goods such as computers.

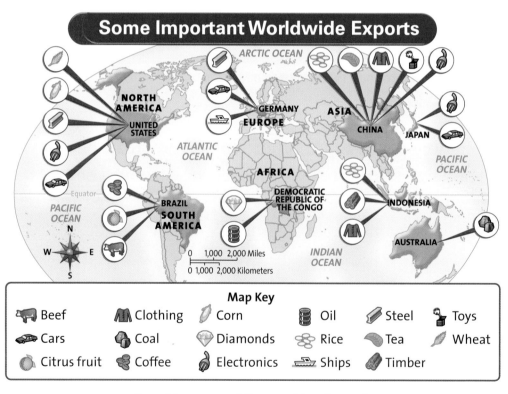

Countries around the world sell goods.

10

Airplanes carry goods around the world.

Countries use transportation technology to ship goods. They send goods by boat, by airplane, by train, and by truck.

In the past, people had to meet to buy and sell goods. Today, people can order goods by telephone. Many people use the Internet to buy and sell goods.

READING CHECK **MAIN IDEA AND DETAILS** **How do countries ship goods?**

Activity 1

Match the word to its meaning.

technology   invention

economy   communication

goods   Internet

service

1. the sharing of information

2. the use of new tools and ideas

3. something that is made for the first time

4. a system that links computers around the world

5. things that can be bought or sold

6. the way a community makes and uses goods and services

7. work that someone does for someone else

Activity 2

Look at the list of vocabulary words. Categorize the words in a chart like the one below. Then use a dictionary to learn the definitions of the words you do not know.

technology	invention	economy
communication	goods	Internet
service	demand	import
economy	international trade	
e-commerce	supply	
e-mail	trade	
export	transportation	

	I Know	Sounds Familiar	Don't Know
technology			✓
economy		✓	
Invention	✓		

Activity 3

Complete each sentence. Use words from the list.

technology	invention
economy	communication
goods	Internet
service	

1. The _____ of a country is the way it makes and uses goods.

2. Doctors provide a _____.

3. The telephone was an important _____.

4. Computers are one kind of _____.

5. People use the telephone for _____.

6. _____ are either made or grown.

7. I use the _____ to send e-mail.

Activity 4

Think about the definition of each word. Then use the word in a sentence that shows its meaning.

1. technology

2. economy

3. goods

4. service

5. invention

6. communication

7. Internet

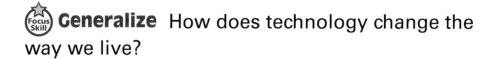 **Generalize** How does technology change the way we live?

Vocabulary

1. List two kinds of **communication**.

Recall

2. What did Josephine Cochran invent?

3. How do banks use computers?

4. What do students use to take part in "the school of the air?"

Critical Thinking

5. How might the world be different without transportation technology?

Activity

Make a Poster Make a poster about technology. Show ways people use technology around the world. Share your poster with the class.

Photo credits Front cover: © Royalty-Free/Corbis; 2, Hisham F Ibrahim/Photodisc Green/Getty Images; 3, Peter Byron/PhotoEdit; 4, Jack Kurtz/The ImageWorks; 5, Barbara Stitzer/PhotoEdit; 6, Judy Rosella Edwards/Ecolitgy Communications; 7, Bettmann/Corbis; 8, Photodisc Blue/Getty Images; 9, Peter Arnold, Inc./Alamy; 11, Bob Krist/Corbis